The Rich–Poor
Divide

Teresa Garlake

Thomson Learning • New York

Global Issues

Closing the Borders
Genetic Engineering
The Rich–Poor Divide
Terrorism
United Nations: Peacekeeper?

First published in the United States in 1995 by
Thomson Learning
New York, NY

Published simultaneously in Great Britain by
Wayland (Publishers) Ltd.

Library of Congress Cataloging-in-Publication Data
Garlake, Teresa.
  The rich – poor divide / Teresa Garlake.
      p.   cm.—(Global issues series)
  Includes bibliographical references and index.
  ISBN 1-56847-336-2
  1. Poverty—Developing countries—Case
studies. 2. Poverty—Case studies. 3. Wealth—
Case studies. I. Title. II. Series: Global issues
(Thomson Learning)
HC59.72.P6G37   1995
339.2—dc20   95-4703

Printed in Italy

Acknowledgments
The author would like to thank Oxfam and Save the
Children Fund for access to the case studies
included in this book. The stories of Haliman and
Joaquin were first told in *Children at Crisis Point*,
published by Save the Children.

Cover picture: People begging outside a temple in
Ho Chi Minh City, Vietnam.
Title page picture: A shantytown in Bombay, India.
Contents page picture: The lifestyle of a wealthy
white woman contrasts with that of a poor black
worker at the Vaal Agricultural Show, Vereeniging,
South Africa.

Picture acknowledgments

Eye Ubiquitous 4, 55, 56 (David
Cumming); Robert Harding 19
(Hist. Picture SVC.), 29 (G.
Hellier), 48; Impact 9 (Paul
Forster), 10 (1988 Marilyn
Humphries), 11, 18 (David Reed),
20 (Bruce Stephens), 42 (Rick
Reinhard), 50 (Piers Cavendish);
Link *contents page*, 22 (Ron
Giling), 39 (Colin Shaw); Oxfam 8
(Jeremy Hartley), 24, 25, 26, 34
(Geoff Sayer), 51, 59 (R. O. Cole);
Panos 12, 32 (Chris Stowers), 33
(Tom Learmonth), 35 (Ron Giling),
40 (Jeremy Hartley), 41 (Jeremy
Hartley), 46 (Ron Giling), 54
(Penny Tweedie); Photri (above)
14 (B. Kulik), 14 (below), 16, 21,
37; Topham 30; Tony Stone
Worldwide *cover, title page*, 44
(Ken Biggs); The Wellcome
Institute Library, London 23; Zefa
Picture Library 59.

CONTENTS

WHAT IS THE RICH–POOR DIVIDE?

Wherever we live, we all want to be happy and secure. We all want a standard of living that makes us feel comfortable; we all want the chance to make the best of the opportunities that life offers. We probably all have different ideas about what happiness means, and we may choose very different ways of life. Yet it is having this choice that matters. Money cannot buy happiness, but it does allow people to have some control over their lives.

This man lives on the sidewalk in Calcutta, India. He will probably never wear the expensive suit that is advertised behind him.

The world can be divided into rich and poor. Many poor people are condemned to lead shorter, harsher lives than rich people. Today, one person out of every five lives in absolute poverty, without some of the essentials for human survival—clean drinking water, nutritious food, shelter, or clothing. But being poor is not just about lacking physical things. It's about not being able to make the best of our lives, about being restricted and, often, powerless. And it's not easy to be happy when we are deprived of the things that we need to stay fed, safe, dry, and healthy.

It's hard to imagine why so many people are poor when so many technological advances have been made over the last hundred years. Most people now expect to live longer than ever before. In countries like Ireland and China, where starvation was once common, there is enough food for everyone. The problem is that the benefits of progress have not been equally shared. Our world is split between the haves and the have nots.

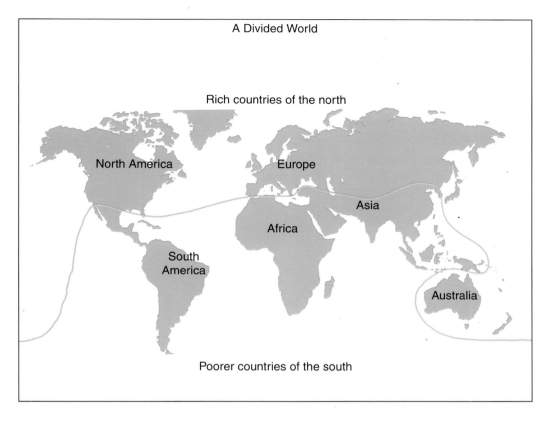

A Divided World

Rich countries of the north

North America

Europe

Asia

Africa

South America

Australia

Poorer countries of the south

The map above shows a line separating the rich countries of the north, from the poor countries of the south (which is sometimes called the Third World or developing world). Not all countries in the north are rich. In Eastern Europe and the former Soviet Union, many people go hungry. The war in the former Yugoslavia, for example, has left many people living in poverty.

There is an invisible line that divides the rich countries of the north from the poor countries of the south.

And not all countries in the south are poor. While some are short of fertile land, many are rich in natural resources such as metals, oil, and rain forests. The problem is that most poor countries do not have the money to develop their wealth. They cannot afford to buy equipment for mining or oil drilling. Those that can have reaped rich rewards. Kuwait has become one of the world's richest countries by exporting oil. Some countries, such as Brazil and Taiwan, are called "newly industrializing" because the number of factories there that produce manufactured goods for export has grown dramatically. However, most people in the south still live off the land, farming for a living.

Fact File

A map showing the differences in consumption in the north and in the south

The richer countries of the north:

Contain 25% of the world's people

Consume 70% of the world's energy

75% of the world's metals

85% of the world's wood

60% of the world's food

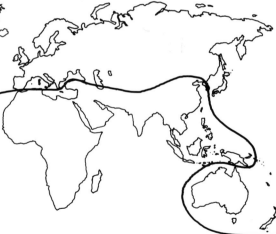

The poorer countries of the south:

Contain 75% of the world's people

Have average incomes $\frac{1}{18}$ that of those in the north

One person out of every six goes hungry

Spend 8% of the world's health care expenditure

Spend 36% of the world's education expenditure

The rich–poor divide in Indonesia and the United States
This chart shows different ways of comparing wealth in
Indonesia and the United States. Similar comparisons
can be made in all parts of the world where there is a
rich–poor divide. Most people agree that poverty is
more than just a question of money. Other factors like
health and education are also important.

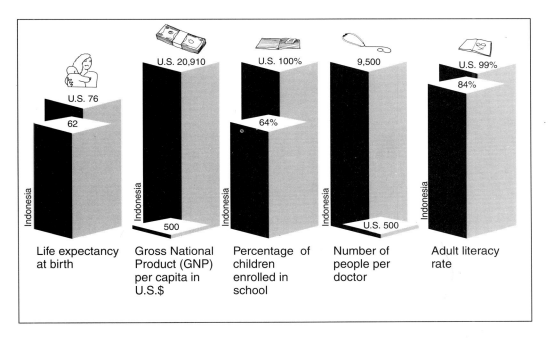

Life expectancy at birth — Indonesia 62, U.S. 76

Gross National Product (GNP) per capita in U.S.$ — Indonesia 500, U.S. 20,910

Percentage of children enrolled in school — Indonesia 64%, U.S. 100%

Number of people per doctor — U.S. 500, Indonesia 9,500

Adult literacy rate — Indonesia 84%, U.S. 99%

Indonesia is by no means one of the world's poorest
countries, but standards of living there are still low
compared to the United States. Most Indonesians are
farmers. However, in recent years Indonesia's economy
has favored industrialization. Today, mines and oil
fields exploit the country's mineral wealth; plantations
grow rubber, tea, coffee, and other crops for export;
factories manufacture parts that will be transported to
rich countries and made into other goods. Foreign
investment brings jobs to some Indonesians; however,
their working conditions are often very poor and their
wages low. Because most factories are owned by
multinational companies from richer countries, much of
Indonesia's wealth does not stay to benefit the people
who live there. The profit goes back to the countries
abroad rather than staying in the Indonesian economy.

A bar graph showing a
few of the many
differences between the
United States and
Indonesia.

Widi, age 12, lives in Bandung, Indonesia

Widi's parents work in a factory, but they do not make a living wage. Their wages do not feed the whole family. So, although he is only 12, Widi is one of millions of children who work for a living. Every morning after he has helped his mother clean the house, Widi rides his bicycle to the bus terminal in the city center. There he works shining shoes.

It is hard work shining shoes, and sometimes Widi does not bring home any money at all. If it is raining, people hurry to get indoors—there's no point in stopping to have their shoes cleaned because they will get wet and dirty again.

Child workers like Widi (above) are often not included in the official employment figures. Yet child labor in cities is on the increase.

Bandung's place in the world (in circle)

Widi sometimes has to miss school because he has to work or help his mother, but he tries not to. Although he's often very tired, he goes straight to school after he gets home from work. "For a shoe-shine boy, I have very high ambitions. I want to get a degree in agriculture so that I can make my homeland more productive."

As well as rich and poor countries, Widi's story shows that there are rich and poor people within countries. Compared to the factory owner's children, Widi has limited opportunities. His job takes time away from school, homework, and playing with his friends. He has more obstacles to overcome before he can achieve his ambitions.

Widi lives in relative poverty, a condition that affects people even in the richest countries, including the United States. Although movies and television shows give the impression that all Americans are rich, this is not the case.

A shoe shiner at work in Indonesia. Many families in the poorer countries of the developing world depend on the income that their children bring in.

These children live in a welfare hotel. In New York City there are many homeless people, many of whom are children. There are more than 27,000 people living in temporary shelters, 50,000 people living on the streets, and 100,000 in friends' houses.

New York City's place in the world (in circle)

Shamelion, age nine, lives in Brooklyn, New York

Shamelion lives in the Brooklyn Arms Hotel. It used to be a high-class hotel in a wealthy part of Brooklyn. Over the years, the area became run down and the Brooklyn Arms was turned into a welfare hotel, a place for people who cannot afford housing.

Shamelion does not think much of where she lives. "The ceiling leaks, which makes the apartment damp. The water doesn't always work and there is no central heating. We share two rooms between six of us. It's crazy." It's difficult to concentrate on homework with so little space. Two hundred and sixty-three families live in the hotel, packed on seventeen floors. The building is always noisy and crowded. It doesn't always feel very safe either. Residents complain that drug pushers hang around the corridors, and once a fire almost burned the place down.

Just across the river from Brooklyn lies another side of New York. In the tree-lined residential streets of the Upper East Side, the city's richest people shop in lavish boutiques and eat in expensive restaurants. A meal in New York City can cost up to $100 per person.

(The average monthly income of a worker in Indonesia is $56.) A subway ride away, Wall Street is home to some of the biggest banks in the world, which have influenced the economies of many developing countries.

Widi's and Shamelion's experiences of poverty are different. Because there are different experiences, there are different ways of measuring poverty. People have different opinions about what characterizes poverty or being poor. To some, it could mean not having three meals a day. To others, it could mean going without a vacation or having to turn the heating down in winter. In fact, the characteristics are so difficult to agree upon that many governments do not have official definitions for poverty.

It's also hard to reach a definition because poverty is difficult to assess. Sometimes poverty is obvious, as in people who are suffering from malnutrition or who are sleeping huddled in doorways or foraging in garbage cans for scraps of food. But sometimes poverty is not obvious. It can be hard to tell if an elderly person is having to go without a meal so that he or she can afford to buy a warm coat for winter. In the countries of the south, the poor tend to live far away from the roads that rich people use to travel from town to town. Governments in cities often try to hide poverty. In 1992, the government of the Dominican Republic, an island in the Caribbean, tried to move 50,000 poor families away from the capital so that they would not be seen by tourists.

Many elderly people, like this woman in Swansea, Wales, live in poverty.

Whether it is hidden or not, the rich–poor divide is felt more keenly by some groups than others. Women make up 70 percent of the world's poor. Throughout the world women do 90 percent of the work, yet they own 2 percent of the world's wealth. Women usually work in jobs that pay less than men's jobs. People in minority groups and indigenous peoples also suffer discrimination, which aggravates their situation. In New Zealand, Maoris are four times as likely to be unemployed as non-Maoris. In Germany, people who are refugees or migrant workers suffer from racial discrimination. Those who were born outside the country are twice as likely to be living in poverty. Often when people move to a new place, they have no choice but to accept the lowest-paid jobs.

Where a person lives is important, as well. Three-quarters of poor people in the south live in rural areas. Traditionally, rural areas have fewer schools, health centers, and facilities such as running water in each household than urban areas. People who do not own land are usually the poorest. Without the means to grow their own food, they must work for others. In some seasons, work is not available and they go hungry.

These people in the Dominican Republic are protesting because their houses have been torn down to make room for apartment buildings in which they will not be able to afford to live.

There is evidence of growing divisions between the rich and the poor. Recently, a major survey in Great Britain found that since 1967 average incomes have risen. But when the survey revealed who was benefiting, the figures were alarming. The richest tenth of the population had doubled its income, but the poorest tenth was no better off than it was 25 years ago. A similar pattern is occurring on a global scale. In richer countries, average standards of living are rising slightly. But in Latin America average incomes today are lower than they were in the early 1980s. In large parts of Africa, they have fallen to the levels they were 30 years ago. So where did the divide begin, and why have some countries ended up so poor?

The distribution of wealth
The champagne-glass diagram illustrates the uneven distribution of wealth. The richest fifth of the world's population consumes more than the remaining four-fifths of the world put together.

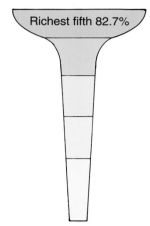

Each horizontal band represents one-fifth of the world's population: the wider it is, the greater the wealth.

Source: *UNDP Human Development Report,* 1994

Media Watch

Who is responsible?
"How are we going to work to develop our community if there is nothing to eat before we go to work and there is nothing left when we get home?"

Amado Assibi, farmer, Ghana, 1993

"The poor, sick, and homeless who roam city streets are not the citizens or products simply of New York or Los Angeles or Detroit or Chicago. They are America's poor, sick and homeless. America has forgotten its collective responsibility to them."

The New York Times, *May 1992*

"The worst scenario is people not feeling responsible for each other, and yes, this is happening."

Radboud Engbersen, a social worker in Holland. Quoted in The Economist, *July 30, 1994.*

HOW DID THE GAP WIDEN?

There have always been divisions between rich and poor people, but the economic gaps that now exist between countries have appeared more recently. We need to look back in history to find out why.

In the fifteenth century, the first explorers from Europe to reach Africa and the Americas were impressed by what they found. The kingdom of Benin, in modern-day Nigeria, had been at its height since 1440. The skills of the city's metal workers were far better than any the Europeans had seen before. In 1498, when the Portuguese landed in east Africa, they were surprised by the wealth and comfort of people living along the coast. They also heard of kingdoms farther inland, like Great Zimbabwe, where craftspeople worked in gold, copper, and iron.

When Europeans like Christopher Columbus (pictured right) arrived in the Americas, indigenous people were forced from their lands. Today their descendants form one of the poorest groups in society.

Pottery and glass were imported from as far away as China. In Central America, the Aztec and Inca kingdoms had been built up over hundreds of years. Early Spanish visitors reached an Inca empire that stretched more than 2,500 miles along the Pacific coast of South America. They saw large road networks and terraces in the mountains that made more land available for growing food. The remains of lavish Aztec and Inca temples can still be seen today. For several hundred years, the north and south met through trading luxury goods such as wool, gold, ivory, and spices. The divisions between areas of the world were not that extreme. But all this changed.

The discovery of America

In 1492, Christopher Columbus, an Italian explorer funded by Spain, landed in the Caribbean. He thought he had found a new western trade route and arrived in India, and so he called the people he met Indians. This is why Europeans called the region the West Indies.

In the first half of the sixteenth century, the Spaniards conquered the Americas, using guns and horses, which the indigenous people had never seen. Their ships carried gold back to Europe. After they had melted down all the gold in the Aztec and Inca treasuries, the Spaniards forced the Indians to dig for more in dangerous mines. Millions of them died from overwork. Millions more were killed or caught fatal diseases brought by the Spaniards. Within a few years, whole indigenous populations had been virtually wiped out.

The Spaniards also brought crops like sugarcane to the Americas and set up plantations. However, so many indigenous peoples had died that they needed more workers.

Media Watch

Celebration or mourning?
The year 1992 was the 500th anniversary of Christopher Columbus's landing in the Americas. People had very different views on the event. Some stressed how the European settlers, who followed Columbus, brought wealth and prosperity to the continent. Others stressed that the Europeans were responsible for the deaths of many indigenous people. Instead of prosperity, the Europeans brought guns, diseases, and the slave trade.

"Here we will not celebrate the five hundred years. It was a massacre and we will mourn it. And we will remember that the massacre, the conquest, continues to this day."

A Mayan Catholic priest speaking in Guatemala in 1992. The Maya are the largest group of indigenous people in Guatemala.

"We need those old virtues pioneered by Columbus nearly five hundred years ago. Christopher Columbus embodies many qualities that can help us: courage, intelligence, perseverance, and vision."

A former administrator of the aid program of the U.S. government, 1992

The African slave trade

The European settlers turned to Africa to find workers, and the slave trade began. Over the next two hundred years, more than 20 million Africans were transported across the Atlantic Ocean. Many died before they reached their destination.

The slave trade was very profitable for European merchants, but it was a terrible abuse of the human rights of the Africans who were transported. Cloth and guns from Europe were exchanged for slaves. In the Americas, slaves worked on plantations, growing raw materials such as sugar, tobacco, rice, and cotton. These were shipped to Europe and sold for large profits. Businessmen in such towns as Bristol and Liverpool in England and Amsterdam in Holland grew very rich.

Slaves landing from a Dutch ship in Jamestown, Virginia.

The trade triangle that supported the slave trade

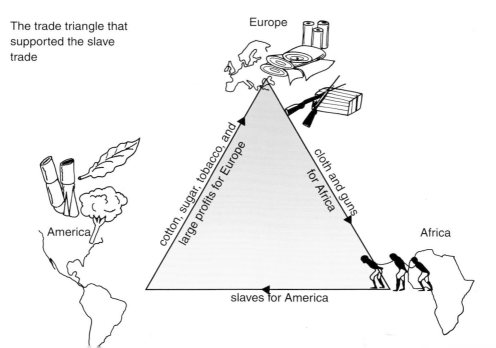

Europe

cotton, sugar, tobacco, and large profits for Europe

cloth and guns for Africa

America

Africa

slaves for America

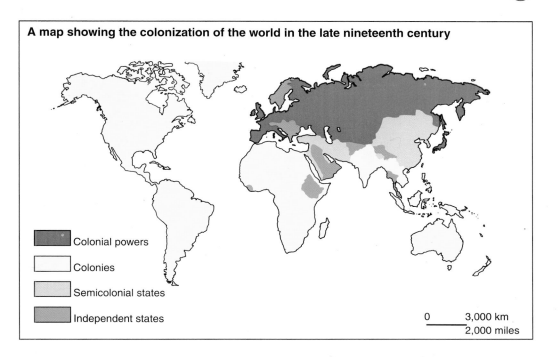

A map showing the colonization of the world in the late nineteenth century

Colonial powers

Colonies

Semicolonial states

Independent states

0   3,000 km
     2,000 miles

Most countries in the south were at one time colonies of European states. Today most are independent, but the effects of colonialism are still apparent.

In these towns today, many of the buildings date from this period.

Money from the slave trade allowed Europe to become richer. It enabled the industrial revolution to take place by paying for new factories and machines to be built. As Europe's wealth grew toward the end of the nineteenth century, European governments began to take over countries in Africa and Asia, using force to gain control. The colonies were a useful marketplace to sell the goods produced in European factories. They were also rich in raw materials, such as coal and gold, that were exported to Europe. Many of the world's poor countries today used to be colonies.

The colonial powers did not want competition from the local industries that already existed in the colonies. India had a thriving cotton industry, but this was swiftly broken down. The British government taxed Indian cloth so heavily that it became cheaper for people in India to export raw, unprocessed cotton. This was woven into cloth in British mills and then sold back to India. Within a few years, Indian cotton producers went out of business, while Great Britain was richer.

Although these events happened a long time ago, their effects are still felt.

A woman hoeing cotton in northwest Tanzania

Kabula, a cotton farmer in Tanzania

Kabula is a farmer who lives in Tanzania. She grows cotton, which has been one of her country's main exports since colonial times. It would be very difficult for Kabula to grow other crops, because it takes time to change from one product to another, and there is no guarantee that growing something different would bring in more money.

Every year, when Kabula sells her crop, she earns enough money to buy herself one brightly colored kanga, which is a piece of cloth traditionally worn by women and men in Tanzania. But Kabula grows enough cotton to make 720 kangas. She often wonders why she gets so little money for all her hard work.

Kabula has to grow cotton, but she has no control over what she gets paid. "Cotton is the only cash crop we grow around here," she explains, "and we have to grow something for cash in order to pay local taxes, to buy books for my brothers and sisters who are still in school, and to buy essentials like salt, shoes, and clothes."

Millions of farmers in developing nations are poor because they are not paid a living wage for what they grow.

The solution—revolution, industrialization, or borrowing

The question of why people like Kabula and others are caught in a poverty trap has occupied many thinkers. One of the most influential of these was a German political philosopher named Karl Marx.

In the 1850s, Marx was angered by the conditions of life for working people in Great Britain. He believed that the industrial revolution could bring an end to poverty, but only if everyone was able to share in the profits. Marx noticed that a few rich people owned the machinery and factories. Most people were poor. They had no choice but to work for very low wages. Factory owners wanted to make profits, and the more they exploited workers, the bigger their profits would be. Marx believed that such inequality was wrong. He was sure that eventually workers would protest and overthrow the factory owners in a revolution. After that, everybody would own the factories together and a new, equal society would be formed. This would be a communist society.

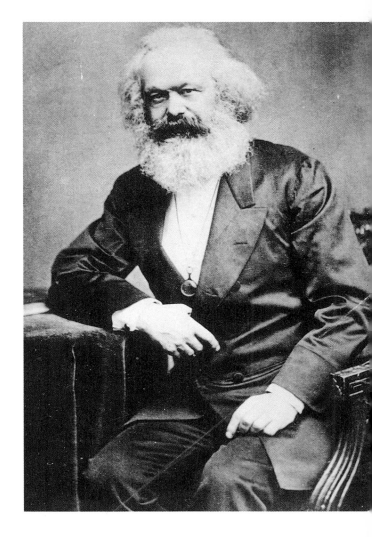

Karl Marx, who wanted to build a new society where everyone was equal

Marx's ideas are still implemented today. Some countries, such as China, Vietnam, Angola, and the former Soviet Union, have tried to put his ideas into practice and bring about equality for their people. However, in practice, working people in communist countries have remained poor while government officials live wealthy lifestyles. Some think that this partly caused the breakup of the Soviet Union.

Other thinkers have had different ideas from Marx's. In the 1950s and 1960s, economists believed that if poor countries followed the same path as richer countries, standards of living would improve. Industrialization was seen as a sign of progress and wealth. As countries grew richer, the benefits of success would trickle down from the rich to the poor.

Mexican workers protest exploitation by the rich.

Countries in the south are also poor because of debt. In the 1970s countries in the south borrowed money from the north, particularly from its large, commercial banks and the International Monetary Fund (IMF). They used the money to pay for education and health services and to industrialize. Some leaders misused the money and spent it on projects that did not benefit the poor. President Ferdinand Marcos of the Philippines borrowed millions of dollars to build luxurious private palaces, which are still being paid for by Filipino people today.

In the mid-1980s, interest rates rose. The cost of borrowing became higher and to pay off their debts countries needed to earn more by exporting more raw materials. But because prices for goods like cotton had fallen, they received less money for what they sold. Many poor countries still owe huge debts.

Today, more and more people believe that the rich and poor countries of the world share a common future. The world is sometimes called a "global village." If rich countries do not tackle the problem of poverty, it will be impossible to maintain peace and stability in the world and protect the environment. Everybody, rich and poor, will suffer. But will countries join together to end poverty? Whatever happens, while the rich–poor divide continues to exist, Kabula and millions of people like her will still feel the effects of poverty.

Fact File

The effects of trade and debt on poverty

Trade: 85 percent of Africa's earnings come from the sale of raw materials such as gold, diamonds, and gravel and cash crops such as cotton and coffee. When the prices paid for raw materials fall, people in Africa become poorer. Prices in 1995 were generally lower than they were in 1980. This means people in rich countries, who do not rely on the sale of raw materials, can buy more, but people in Africa don't see the benefits.

In 1994, several miles underground, South African gold miners work for only $160 a month.

Debt: To pay off their debts, governments are forced to spend less. In some countries, the government is no longer able to pay for state education. In Kenya, primary education used to be free. Now it costs $44 a month. Fees in secondary schools have doubled from $90 to $180. The average income in Kenya is about $350 a year. Without a basic education it is difficult for people to escape from poverty.

LOOKING AT THE EFFECTS— HEALTH AND EDUCATION

In many of the industrialized countries, staying healthy and going to school are taken for granted. If someone gets sick, a doctor is close by. People there can expect to live long lives, with all the food they need. They can also read, which means that they will have better chances when they look for jobs.

It's much harder for people who are poor to overcome disadvantages and change their lives for the better. Without the opportunities that go with health and education, they are more likely to remain trapped by the rich–poor divide.

People who come from wealthy backgrounds tend to live longer: they get more to eat, are healthier, and live in better housing conditions. In Great Britain, babies born into the poorest 5 percent of families are twice as likely to die in their first year as babies born into the richest 5 percent of families. In Canada, the indigenous Inuit people have a life expectancy that is five years shorter than that of other Canadians.

Healthy and happy— young people in a carnival street parade in Holland

In the south, most people still die from illnesses that are caused by unclean water or malnutrition. These are often called "diseases of poverty" and they could easily be prevented if more money were available. Diarrhea, for example, is a simple but dangerous illness caused by dirty water. Every year it takes the lives of more than 4.6 million children. If everyone had safe, clean water to drink, 80 percent of sickness in the world could be avoided. It has been said that it is better to judge the health of a nation by counting the number of water pumps than the number of hospital beds.

Over the past few generations, standards of living have improved. People—even wealthy people—in the early twentieth century may not have had bathrooms or indoor lavatories in their houses. They might have seen illnesses such as polio. Diseases of poverty were common in rich countries. In the 1850s, tuberculosis (TB) was the largest cause of death in Great Britain. Gradually, living standards improved. Diets became healthier, and houses were not as overcrowded or damp.

Visiting a tuberculosis clinic in Pennsylvania in the 1940s. This disease used to be much more common, but improvements in living conditions have made it rare in richer countries.

Water and sanitation systems became more advanced. There was also medical progress. Immunizations, which became common in the 1950s, prevented many deaths from diseases such as polio or TB. Over time, TB began to disappear. Today, it is very rare in the north (although it is reappearing among people who live on the streets). Improvements in living conditions have meant that death rates have fallen considerably. Wherever they live, poor people are more likely to

A 31-year-old sugar worker in the Philippines, who has been suffering from tuberculosis for ten years without any treatment, demands access to a clinic with a doctor.

suffer from illness. They are more likely to live in polluted areas and have less money to spend on wholesome food or less land to grow it on. A person who is sick cannot work. In a family without savings, this could be the start of serious problems. Without money the family can't get food and is more likely to become malnourished. Malnutrition makes children especially vulnerable to illness. If they do become sick, buying medicines will make the family even poorer. It becomes very difficult to escape from the consequences of poverty.

Valeria, a community health worker, lives in La Bandera, Santiago, Chile

Valeria has seen how closely poverty and illness are linked. She lives in La Bandera, a shantytown on the edge of Santiago, the capital of Chile. Many families who live there have moved from the countryside. With great skill, they have built their houses themselves from materials that they have found—corrugated iron, wood, plastic, and even flattened tin cans. La Bandera is a crowded area. Although people try to keep the streets clean, it's difficult because there are no sanitation facilities. Valeria has noticed that illness is very common, especially among children. "We don't eat well, we live in bad houses, we don't have water," explains Valeria. "That's why people get sick. It's not just bad luck that people suffer; there are reasons."

Valeria decided that things needed to change and, together with six other women in her neighborhood, set up a group called Llareta, after a flower that blooms without water in the desert. "I began to learn about nutrition and how good health is connected with everything. I learned that the house has to be clean, that it should have a decent floor,

Valeria takes her health message to the people of the shantytown where she lives.

Media Watch

"Water is very scarce, I have to go a long way to fetch it. There is no school, no hospital—the nearest one is a maternity hospital, but there is no doctor. I cannot use the private clinic—I have no money."

Basidia, who lives in Santo Domingo in the Dominican Republic

"It's cold and damp in this house. We just got a heater for the children's room that took years to get. I've got bronchitis and so have the children."

Julie, who lives in England

and proper walls." Valeria and her friends teach the community how to stay healthy. "We have to help people prevent illness, because they don't have the money to be ill, and there isn't enough medical attention for everyone. We try to teach people how to use their resources better, like buying cheap and nutritious vegetables instead of meat."

Countries in the south, like Chile, do not have as much money to spend on health care as richer countries. They need to think very carefully how to make the best use of what they have. Building hospitals with all the latest technology is expensive. Besides, most people live in the countryside and can't afford to travel very far. More and more governments are setting up small health centers that are within easy reach of most people.

People like Valeria who work in these centers are called community health workers. Their main jobs are to prevent sickness in the first place, by giving

Valeria relaxing at home in La Bandera, Santiago, Chile

people advice on healthy eating and hygiene. As the saying goes, prevention is better than cure. Community health workers do not receive a lot of training, but they know how to treat most common illnesses. They are very dedicated people who are not paid much for their work. Like Valeria, most community health workers usually come from the local neighborhood, so they know the problems of the people with whom they are working.

Literacy

Poor health keeps people in poverty, but so does not being able to read, write, or do simple math. Illiteracy has a profound effect on many people's lives. Illiterate people are not able to read bus timetables or write letters. They are not able to look up numbers in the telephone book, and they might be in danger if they can't read warning signs or labels. Illiterate people often find great difficulty in finding jobs. They are often poorly paid and are sometimes cheated because they can't read contracts. In some countries, only literate citizens are allowed to vote.

Joaquin, age 15, a street vendor in Manila, in the Philippines

Joaquin is one of about a million children who live on the streets of Manila, the capital of the Philippines. In the bustling city center, he makes a living by selling cigarettes to people waiting at the traffic lights. He does not have much time to spend in school. He needs to earn money to survive.

Luckily, Joaquin has found an education that fits in with what he needs. He goes to Bahay Tuluyan, a center especially for street children. There he's learning to read, write, and do simple math. He's also finding out more about things that will help him care for himself better. The center offers courses on the legal rights of street children so that they can deal with harassment, the police, and housing problems. Also, they are given guidance on the best kinds of food to eat, how to keep warm, and where to seek medical attention if they become sick. Being literate will give Joaquin more confidence as he becomes older. He is less likely to be exploited and stands a better chance of escaping from life on the streets.

It is much harder for children like Joaquin, who come from poorer families or have no families, to do well at school. It's more difficult to travel long distances to get there, children may be needed to work at home, and books or uniforms may be too expensive to buy. Children in the south are much less likely to finish their schooling. Fewer girls than boys go to school, because girls' education is thought to be less important. Girls usually are the first to be kept at home to help around the house.

Health and education are building blocks for the future of countries in both the north and the south. They help people take control of their lives and find a way out of poverty. But today, governments in the south have less money to spend on these necessities than they did twenty years ago. That's not because they think their people are unimportant. It's because many countries cannot afford to spend money on services. As populations grow, it becomes even harder to provide enough for everybody.

Fact File

Health and Education

In the north, on average there is one doctor for every 400 people. In the south, there is one doctor for nearly 7,000.

The Republic of Korea, a newly industrializing country, spends $377 per person on health; but Bangladesh can only afford to spend $7 per person.

There are about 100 million children of primary school age in the world who are not going to school.

United Nations Development Program: Human Development Report,

THE POPULATION PUZZLE

Today there are 5.5 billion people in the world. This number has doubled since 1950 and it will increase to 8.5 billion by the year 2025. Some people explain the rich–poor divide by saying that there are just too many people in the world. But is this true?

It is certainly true that some parts of the world support many more people than others. Fertile land, plentiful supplies of water, a comfortable climate, and good road or rail systems all make regions attractive for people to settle. There are other regions with environments that make life very difficult. But it's not just a question of how many people live in a country.

Some countries are much more crowded than others, though having a high population density does not necessarily mean that a country will be poor. Holland, which is a rich country, is the most heavily populated country in the world. If Holland's whole population were spread evenly throughout the country there would be 958 people in every square mile. In Ethiopia, which is very poor, the population density is only 134 people per square mile. Densely populated countries have to share land, food, shelter, and services among more people. This is not a problem for richer countries, which can afford to provide enough for everyone; poorer countries find it much harder.

Rural beauty, yet in Nepal pressure on fertile land in the mountain and hill areas is forcing people to move into areas where the environment is more fragile. It will gradually become harder to make a living from the land.

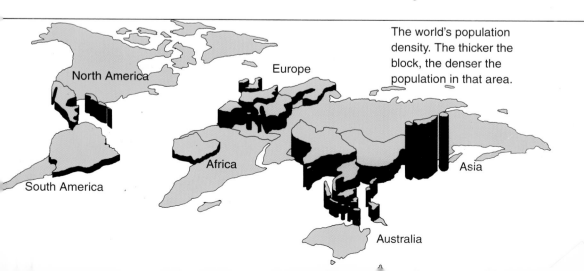

The world's population density. The thicker the block, the denser the population in that area.

North America

Europe

Africa

Asia

South America

Australia

Thomas Malthus (1766–1834)

In 1798, British economist Thomas Malthus published his theory on population growth. He believed that food supplies in Great Britain could not grow as fast as the population. Eventually, he predicted, there would not be enough food for everyone. This would lead to famine, war, and poverty.

Malthus's predictions never came true. One reason for this is that he did not foresee the advances in agriculture that would allow more food to be grown in Great Britain. However, his ideas continue to have a powerful influence. Today, neo-Malthusians, as his followers are called, still argue that high birth rates cause poverty. They say that population growth must be stopped. If not, the earth will run out of natural resources and raw materials. They add that the environment is being destroyed by increasing numbers of people who all need somewhere to live; cities are growing too quickly; and there is mass poverty and unemployment.

The increase in world population since A.D. 1000

Population (billions)

5

4

3

2

1

1000 1100 1200 1300 1400 1500 1600 1700 1800 1900 2000
year

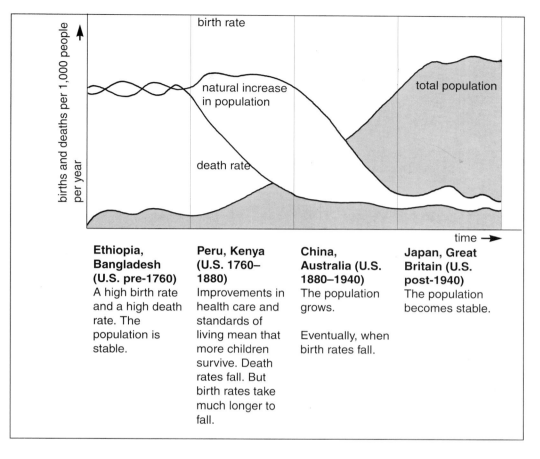

births and deaths per 1,000 people per year

birth rate

natural increase in population

total population

death rate

time →

Ethiopia, Bangladesh (U.S. pre-1760)	Peru, Kenya (U.S. 1760–1880)	China, Australia (U.S. 1880–1940)	Japan, Great Britain (U.S. post-1940)
A high birth rate and a high death rate. The population is stable.	Improvements in health care and standards of living mean that more children survive. Death rates fall. But birth rates take much longer to fall.	The population grows. Eventually, when birth rates fall.	The population becomes stable.

The population cycle

This gloomy picture explains why the population puzzle is a topic of such heated debate. Population is growing fastest in the south, although in recent years birth rates have been falling nearly everywhere. South of the Sahara, in Africa, is the exception. The south is often blamed for its own poverty because of population growth. But we also need to look at how population growth happens.

Many countries in the south today are seeing their death rates fall. As more children survive to become adults, a larger young population is just reaching its child-bearing years. This is why, even if the number of children born in each family is reduced, the population will continue to grow. Eventually, however, the growth will level off as birth rates fall. Populations that go through changes in birth or death rates are said to be in transition.

(Left) Many countries in the south are trying to slow down their population growth. This poster in Vietnam calls on families to have only one child.

All populations go through transition stages. The north has had its own population explosions. Families of several generations ago were much larger than those of today. From the early nineteenth century, the populations in Europe and the United States expanded as standards of living improved. It has only been in the twentieth century that the population has become stable. Today, the south is going through similar changes to those that have happened in the north.

There are good reasons why families in the south tend to have more children. Children in poverty are more likely to become sick and even die. In the south, 100 babies out of every 1,000 die before the age of 5, compared to 15 babies out of 1,000 in the north. Poorer families choose to have more children to increase the chance that some will survive to adulthood.

(Below) Dhaka, the capital of Bangladesh, one of the most densely populated countries of the world. Eight out of every ten people still live in rural areas.

Faith, age 15, lives in Uganda

Having more children has many benefits that Faith, who is 15 years old, can see. She lives with her large family in the lush green hills of Uganda. Faith has two older brothers and four younger brothers and sisters. Like most people in the South, her parents make their living from farming. They wanted to have a lot of children to help them work on their farm. The children all began helping out with chores when they were very young: caring for animals, fetching firewood and water, and helping with weeding. By the time they are ten or eleven years old, children in the south are often earning money.

Faith harvesting the coffee crop on the family farm

All the children in Faith's family have had some schooling. Her parents have tried very hard to pay for school fees, books, and uniforms. These things are very expensive in Uganda, where education is no longer free. Faith left school before she was 11 years old, even though her grades were very good. Now she works as a cleaner in the local hospital. She is helping to pay for the education of her brother William. When he gets a job he will also help the family out with his wages. Faith hopes that she will save enough money to continue her education. "Going to school does matter to me. It is important for me. But my family is important, too. As long as I can work and contribute I don't feel frustrated by that. We just support each other."

For Faith's parents, and many others in the south, children are an important security for the future. When there are no retirement funds or welfare systems, children are needed to take care of their aging parents. If they become sick, Faith's parents will depend on her and the others to work on the farm.

More and more people are suggesting that population growth is a result rather than a cause of poverty. In industrialized nations, they say, population growth has slowed down because people are better off. The same would happen in the south if poverty was ended. It has already been shown that women who have had some education tend to have fewer children. When mothers have more choices and better employment opportunities, their children have better starts in life.

Studies have shown that educated women in Uganda have fewer but healthier children.

Fact File

Expensive children

Children in the north cost their families much more than children in the south. Parents may have to give up work and lose earnings while they care for their children. School trips, music lessons, housing, and clothing bills all cost money. A child in the United States costs its parents tens of thousands of dollars from the time it is born until it is sixteen. In the south, children often start working at a younger age. By their fifteenth birthdays, they have usually earned the equivalent of all the money their family has spent feeding, clothing, and educating them.

The neo-Malthusian view of population is being questioned in other ways. People are asking whether population growth in the south is the real problem after all. Everyone agrees that the earth has limited resources, but we need to look at who uses most of them. Take oil, for example. Oil is used to heat homes and to run machines and as gasoline for cars. In the United States, each person uses, on average, the equivalent of 55 barrels of oil each year. In comparison, the average Bangladeshi uses the equivalent of 3 barrels per year. New York City uses more gasoline in a week than the whole of Africa in a year.

In fact, the population in the south could grow to four times its size and it would still not consume as much as the north. Perhaps overconsumption in the north is the problem, rather than overpopulation in the south. Is it the north, which uses up more than its fair share of resources, that needs to change?

Media Watch

Overpopulation?
"The population problem...is the greatest red herring in the field of world development. By stressing population in such an isolated, simplistic manner we may have lost twenty precious years in solving its number one problem—poverty."

Pierre Pradervand, author and researcher on population

"The greatest single obstacle to the economic and social advancement of the people in the underdeveloped world is rampant population growth."

Robert McNamara, President of the World Bank from 1968 to 1981

FOOD FOR ALL?

Each year, 40 million people die from hunger and many more fall sick because they are suffering from malnutrition. Almost half of the victims are children. It's hard to imagine what this figure means, but it's equal to 300 jumbo jets crashing every single day, with no survivors.

Even the richest countries in the world suffer from drought. In the 1930s land in the United States was commonly overused. Huge areas of fertile land became the dust bowl.

In the midst of such hunger, the world is not short of food. In the 1980s, food production grew much faster than the world's population. There is currently enough food to give everybody 2,500 calories a day, which is 200 more than most people need. Yet one of our most valuable resources is not equally divided. The north, with only a quarter of the world's people, consumes more than half the world's food.

Hunger has always existed, but changes in farming and land ownership have made it a more serious global problem in more recent times. At the beginning of the nineteenth century, parts of southern Africa were noted for their rich food supplies. Yet, by the 1930s, malnutrition was widespread. Colonials forced many farmers off their land. The land was taken over by European settlers who planted cash crops and exported them to earn money. Today the south continues to grow cash crops, which leaves less land to grow food for people to eat.

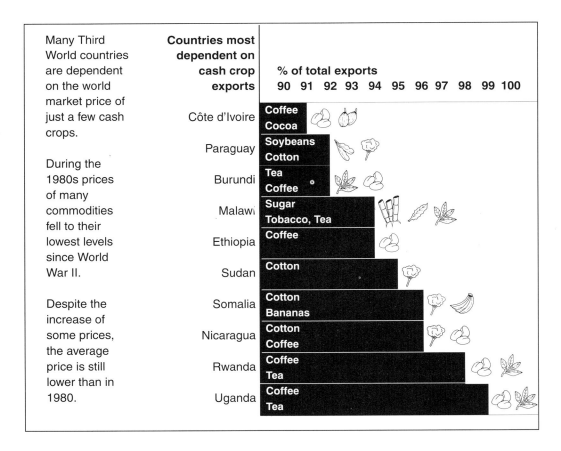

Many Third World countries are dependent on the world market price of just a few cash crops.

During the 1980s prices of many commodities fell to their lowest levels since World War II.

Despite the increase of some prices, the average price is still lower than in 1980.

Countries most dependent on cash crop exports

% of total exports

90 91 92 93 94 95 96 97 98 99 100

Côte d'Ivoire	Coffee / Cocoa
Paraguay	Soybeans / Cotton
Burundi	Tea / Coffee
Malawi	Sugar / Tobacco, Tea
Ethiopia	Coffee
Sudan	Cotton
Somalia	Cotton / Bananas
Nicaragua	Cotton / Coffee
Rwanda	Coffee / Tea
Uganda	Coffee / Tea

Fast food may be tasty but it is usually not healthy.

In the north, families with low incomes often can't afford to buy healthy food, such as fresh fruit or vegetables. They are forced to eat cheaper, processed foods that contain a lot of fat but fewer vitamins. People with unhealthy diets are more likely to suffer from illnesses such as anemia, chest infections, or weight problems. In the south, hunger is more widespread, but this does not mean that everyone is malnourished. Even when there is famine, richer people do not starve. That's because they can afford to buy food at high prices. People do not go hungry because there is no food in the markets, but because the food is priced too high for most consumers.

Sometimes countries are also too poor to buy food for their people. The north does not grow all its own food, but can afford to import it. Food on the supermarket shelves in the north comes from all over the world. Even if the country's harvests fail, people will not go hungry. This is not always true in the south.

Issakha, a farmer in central Chad

Issakha depends on the rain for his food. He has been living in the dry lands of central Chad for 20 years. "When we came here, the area was a good one. If you sowed your fields, you could find plenty of food. For the past eight years, everything has changed. We plow our fields but we can't grow enough food. Even our donkeys can't find grass to eat. Now the area is like the Sahara. Since the drought came it has changed completely. To survive, my wife and I cut dried trees and transport them to the market on our donkeys for sale. I had to sell 22 goats to survive this year."

A web of reasons link together to explain why Issakha, his wife, and their children face hunger. Natural disaster, such as drought or flooding, is the most obvious.

Drought in Chad has forced farmers to eat their supplies of seed. Distributing millet seed will enable farmers to grow their own food again when the rains come.

However, natural disasters do not always lead to food shortages. In 1988, drought hit the Midwest of the United States. Although many farmers went out of business, they did not starve. The farmers and the government were rich enough to prevent famine. Farmers were given money to help them through the difficult times.

Issakha and his family suffer more from natural disaster because they are already poor. They do not have savings or food reserves. Once all their goats are sold and their food eaten, they may have to leave their land in search of food.

Some countries in the south are able to protect their people against food shortages. In Botswana drought is not uncommon. However, the government has been able to build up resources to prevent hunger. Children get extra food when they go to school, and adults can earn money to buy food by working on community projects. A good road and rail system enables food to be moved around the country quickly.

This land was once green with trees. Every year an area of land the size of Ireland is turned into desert.

Environmental damage also causes hunger. Issakha can see the desert spreading every year. As trees are cut down to clear land for crops or to gather fuel, the soil is exposed to wind and rain. Precious soil blows away or is carried off by floods. The land soon begins to lose its fertility. Poverty forces farmers like Issakha to overuse their land. They know that it should be left unplanted, or fallow, for a year, but they need to keep planting to get enough food to eat. They have to clear new land, and the whole process begins again.

José, farmer and member of the Landless People's Movement, Paraiba, Brazil

Because of the rich–poor divide, many people do not have enough to eat, even though there is plenty of food to go around. Brazil is the second-largest agricultural exporter in the world, yet one person out of every three does not have enough to eat. Huge expanses of land are owned by just a few big landowners. Much of this land lies uncultivated. Meanwhile, small farmers, like José and his family, try to scratch a living from land they do not legally own because they cannot afford to buy it. They can be thrown off at any time, even if they are just about to harvest their crops.

Hiring a lawyer, such as Pedro Dalcero in Brazil, may win farmers the right to legal ownership of their land. In Brazil, almost 11 million farmers do not have enough land to support their families.

One day José found out how risky this way of life is. "I worked for a landowner for 20 years and then he just threw me off the land. He could do that because he was powerful." José and other landless families knew that they needed land in order to survive. Together they set up the Landless People's Movement. One night they moved to an abandoned farm that they called *Esperança*, meaning "hope." They brought whatever they could from their old houses and soon built new ones. At first, they were frightened, waiting for the police to come to move them on. But they planted food crops and began to bring the land back to life.

The Landless People's Movement also hired lawyers to establish legal ownership of the land. José hopes that this will mean an end to hunger for him and his family. "We came here for land. We didn't come to get rich. People were born from the land and must live from it."

War is another reason that people go hungry. Armies know that everyone needs food, so they often use it as a weapon, keeping it from people who need it. Crops are destroyed in conflict and farmers are forced to leave their fields untended.

The rich–poor divide results in hunger. In Chad, Issakha does not have the resources to protect himself and his family from drought. In Brazil, landless people are unable to feed themselves. However, it can be a different story. Famine used to be common in China in the 1930s, when the country had one of the world's highest death rates. Today, food and other resources are divided much more equally, and there has been no starvation recorded in China since the 1950s.

Many families in the south continue to seek an escape from land shortages, war, and hunger. They are moving to the cities, in search of a new life.

Media Watch

Looking at hunger
"Starvation is the characteristic of some people not having enough to eat. It is not the characteristic of there not being enough food to eat."

Amar'tya Sem, Indian economist, 1981

"If we were to keep a minute of silence for every person who died in 1982 because of hunger, we would not be able to celebrate the coming of the twenty-first century because we would still have to remain silent."

Fidel Castro, President of Cuba, March 1983

THE GROWTH OF CITIES

Cities and large towns leave visible signs of their growth. Some of the oldest buildings in a city will be in the center. On the outskirts will be new suburbs, built for an expanding population. There might be large building sites surrounding the city as it spreads its way into the countryside. Roads and railroads allow the suburbs to stretch even farther. Growing cities are not unusual. In fact, the world's urban population is more than three times the size it was in 1950.

In the north, urbanization was quite a slow process, which took place over about two hundred years. In the eighteenth century, changes in farming methods and inventions such as Jethro Tull's seed drill enabled more food to be produced by fewer people. At the same time, landlords also began to fence in common land that previously had been used by everyone. People who were thrown off their land were forced to move to the towns and cities in search of work. They provided the labor force that was needed for the new factories and mines of the industrial revolution.

A city on the move—Los Angeles at dusk

Fact
File

The growth of cities
In the south, the growth of cities has taken place much more quickly than in the north. Today there are 20 cities in the world with more than 8 million people. Fourteen of these are in the south, whereas in 1950 there were none. Many countries in the south have one city that is much larger than any others. These have often grown up from ports or trading centers that were set up during colonial times for exporting goods from the country.

Cities in size order (includes entire metropolitan areas)	1991 – Population (in millions)	2000 – Population (in millions, projected)
Tokyo-Yokohama, Japan	27.245	29.971
Mexico City, Mexico	20.899	27.872
São Paulo, Brazil	18.701	25.354
Seoul, South Korea	16.792	21.976
New York, New York	14.625	14.648
Bombay, India	12.101	15.357
Calcutta, India	11.898	14.088
Rio de Janeiro, Brazil	11.688	14.169
Buenos Aires, Argentina	11.657	12.911
Moscow, Russia	10.446	11.121
Manila, Philippines	10.156	12.911
Los Angeles, California	10.130	10.714
Cairo, Egypt	10.099	12.512
Jakarta, Indonesia	9.882	12.804
Tehran, Iran	9.779	14.251
London, Great Britain	9.115	8.574
Delhi, India	8.778	11.849
Paris, France	8.720	8.803
Karachi, Pakistan	8.014	11.299
Lagos, Nigeria	7.998	12.528

Cities have always acted as magnets, drawing people who come in search of better opportunities. There are greater chances of finding work there. Families believe that their children will benefit because there are more schools and health centers. But most people move to cities because they have little choice. They may have been thrown off their land or forced to leave their homes because of war, natural disaster, or environmental damage.

The rich–poor divide is most obvious in cities, where wealth and luxury are on display beside extreme poverty. Many cities in the south are in fact two cities. In the thriving, cosmopolitan city centers the newest imported goods and the latest records are for sale. On the outskirts lie shantytowns where most people live. People here cannot afford to buy land. Families have to build their homes in the worst areas, on hillsides or next to rivers that flood when it rains. There's often no clean water or sanitation; electricity is a luxury.

Governments tend to turn a blind eye to the shantytowns, refusing to provide services. This is often because they do not want to encourage more migration from rural areas. Yet despite these obstacles, the communities that exist there are often very strong, and people work hard to help each other.

A recycled home—this family in Manila, the Philippines, has built its house in a shantytown out of found materials.

Haliman, age eight, lives in New Delhi, India

Haliman and her family live in New Delhi, the capital of India. They used to live far out in the countryside. The family had farmed a small piece of land for generations, although they did not own it. "Life in our village was fun," says Haliman. "All day long I played with my cousins—they are all girls, you know. We climbed trees and picked mangos. We went for rides in my uncle's bullock cart. We made dolls with wheat straw and cloth, and the dolls would marry and have children!"

One day the landlord threw the family off the land. They had to move to the city to try and earn a new living. It is especially difficult for poor families like Haliman's to migrate to cities. They have no money saved, and there is no welfare system to provide food or shelter. With so many people chasing the few jobs, the chances of finding work are slim. New arrivals have to take whatever jobs they can find and end up working long hours for very little money. Work conditions are often dangerous and workers may be let go without any warning. Many people in cities, both in the north and south, end up working in the "informal economy"—as shoe shiners, window cleaners, or even beggars.

Haliman making roti (bread) for the family meal in New Delhi, India

Haliman's family was luckier than some and found work on a construction site. Her mother and older sister, Aapa, work all day carrying ten bricks at a time on their heads. Her father has a better job as a stonemason on a construction site on the other side of the city. It's too far away and costs too much to come home more than twice a week. He always arrives very late, so Haliman rarely sees him even then.

Haliman lives on the construction site. It's very overcrowded and most families share only one room. It's not worth spending money on building a permanent house, because jobs are so insecure and families, may have to move very quickly. There are no sanitation facilities and people often catch diseases. Haliman has to carry water from a communal tap near the construction site. Lots of people share the one tap, so she always hopes that she does not have to wait in line for too long.

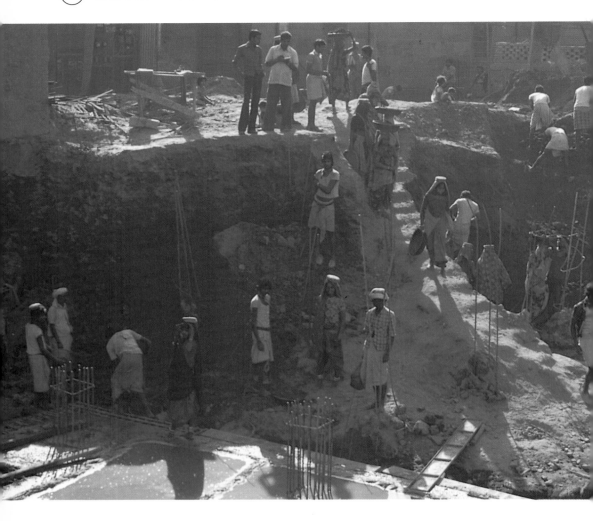

Life for Haliman has changed since coming to the city. She's only eight years old, but she says she's too old to play with dolls now. Instead she takes care of her younger sisters Hasina, who is three, and Jumerati, who is still a baby. She cooks the meals for her mother and sisters and looks after the house. Every day she also spends some hours at a center that has been set up for children like her. Workers there watch Hasina and Jumerati, and this gives Haliman a few hours to play and take some classes.

Many cities have grown because of industrialization. When India became an independent country in 1947, the prime minister, Jawaharlal Nehru, began to industrialize it. Migration to the cities fed a growing

Children are often hired on construction sites along with their parents. The hard physical labor stunts their growth. Their futures are not promising.

Fact File

City Life
Between 1950 and 1990, the population of the world's towns and cities grew more than twice as fast as rural areas.

- In 1950, 29 people out of every 100 lived in a city. In 1990, 45 people out of every 100 lived in a city.

- In Asia one in every four city dwellers lives in a shantytown. In Africa, two out of every three do.

- Pollution in cities has always been a problem. One smog in London lasted from November 1879 to the following March. Today, breathing the air in Mexico City, one of the most polluted in the world, has the same effect as smoking 40 cigarettes a day.

demand for people to work in industry. Today, India has one of the world's richest economies. Factories produce just about everything, from microwave ovens to Rover cars. But industry has not created the jobs that many expected. As technology has improved, machines perform more and more tasks that used to be done by hand. Most Indians still earn their livings from agriculture, which is not as highly mechanized. While wealth has been generated by industrialization, it stays in the hands of a few richer people and out of reach of those like Haliman.

In northern cities, too, evidence of the rich–poor divide is easy to see. Industries are declining and unemployment is rising. Rotterdam, Holland, has a vast harbor where machines rather than people now do the heavy work of loading and unloading the ships. Many workers have lost their jobs, and today there are three Dutch people who live off state benefits for every four people with full-time jobs.

Between 1950 and the mid-1970s, nearly a quarter of the population —mainly richer white people—left New York City to move to the suburbs and outlying towns, in what became known as "white flight." The poor were left behind.

Inner cities in the north are often neglected areas, with poor housing and roads that have fallen into disrepair. Richer people, attracted by the open space and greenery, have moved out to suburbs. New companies have set up their businesses in industrial parks on the city outskirts. People who remain in the inner city often face problems associated with poverty. There is fierce competition for jobs. Crime rates are higher. Some groups, such as the elderly, are especially lonely and isolated. Single parents and people from ethnic minorities find it hard to escape the urban poverty trap.

Despite these difficulties, the world's cities continue to grow. The United Nations estimates that by 2020, two out of every three people will live in a city. The experience of Haliman has shown that urbanization is not an easy answer to poverty. In fact, far from ending poverty, living in cities often places poor people in situations of greater hardship and insecurity.

WHAT CAN BE DONE?

Few people would disagree that poverty is an injustice that should be ended. It's more difficult to agree on what should be done. Some people argue that governments should provide for the poor by taxing the rich more and by giving aid to needy countries. Other people argue that individuals should try to help people living in poverty by giving to charities. Some charities have sponsored walks or bike rides; some schools raise money for charitable causes. The desire to help others is a basic human response.

Giving to charity can provide real support to those in need. Most people are lucky enough not to have to rely on charity to provide them with food, shelter, or clothing. But all of us have received assistance or aid in one form or another, from family or the government.

Active support of charity events helps to raise money and awareness of the injustice of the rich–poor divide.

Some people do not have to pay for their education, transportation to school, or school meals. Unemployed people in the north often receive state benefits while they look for jobs. Richer people receive aid, too. Home owners often pay less in taxes if they have a mortgage.

Many people say that poverty in the north is not the problem it was a hundred years ago, so there is no longer a need for charities. Others insist that poverty is still a major problem and that governments should be doing more to combat it. By expecting charities to raise money for the poor, to buy hospital equipment, or to provide support to the sick or elderly, they say the government is avoiding its responsibilities.

It is true that governments can give poor people the bricks to build their own futures. They can create jobs and training opportunities. This is especially important for groups that suffer discrimination. Governments can also provide benefits to keep fewer people from living in poverty. In richer countries the government can afford to provide more for its people, but money still has to come from somewhere. Getting rich people to pay more taxes is one way of making sure that money is more evenly distributed, but some people argue that high taxes prevent money from being reinvested in the economy. High taxes are also not popular with the wealthy.

In many countries, governments are trying to end the poverty that their people face. However, this is not easy.

The United Nations in session. The United Nations with its 34 specialized agencies was set up after World War II in the hope of making the world a more secure place. If this ideal is to be achieved, global inequality must be ended.

Debt and the world trade system work together to widen the rich–poor divide. Latin America and the countries in Africa that lie south of the Sahara spend a quarter of the money that they earn from their exports to pay off their debts. Until they have more money available, countries in the south will not be able to help their people.

One way to ease the poverty in the south would be if the north forgave poorer countries their debts. In 1992, the south paid $160 billion to the north to cover debts. The rich–poor divide would also be lessened if countries in the south were paid a better price for the raw materials that they produce. Kabula's story in chapter two told how her life is affected by low cotton prices. Over the last few years, the prices of raw materials have fallen dramatically, but the prices of manufactured goods have not. Today, countries in the south need to export far more in order to buy essential products such as oil, machinery, and fertilizers.

Aid

Aid is a weapon in the fight against poverty. The type of aid and the way in which it is given are very important. Food from soup kitchens provides people who live on the streets much-needed meals. But hand-outs can be detrimental. Aid can sometimes make those who receive it feel inferior or powerless. Most people who live on the streets would probably much rather be given jobs that would allow them to buy their own food. Soup kitchens are a short-term solution. People also need the kind of aid or help that would give them the chance to take control of their own lives.

These homeless and mentally ill people are receiving hot meals in a church. It is a welcome support, but will it help them become independent in the long run?

Aid is also given by one country to another. Newspapers and television often give the impression that all flows from the north to the south. In reality, it's a different picture. Payments on debts that the south pays the north are more than twice the amount that the south receives in aid. Countries in the north receive aid too. After World War II, as part of the Marshall Plan, the United States gave vast quantities of aid to rebuild

Europe and get trade moving again. Today, many parts of Europe receive aid from the European Community, which is used to restore areas that have suffered from economic decline. Southern countries also give aid to other southern countries.

A rusty truck in French Guiana shows that aid is not always useful. If local people had been consulted, they might have preferred more appropriate, local technology.

Most aid to the south is provided by governments in the north. But how is it used and who really benefits? Government aid is usually tied, which means that there are conditions restricting the way it can be used. For example, a country that is given agricultural aid may be told to use the money to buy a certain type of tractor produced in the north. The tractor might not be the

best for local conditions; it might be expensive to run, and local farm laborers might lose their jobs if machinery were to take over. The country that receives aid may also have to use the skills of foreign experts, even though local people can do the job just as well. In this way, donor countries benefit from giving tied aid. More jobs are created in the north in the manufacturing industries that make the equipment given through tied aid.

Sometimes expensive aid projects do not help the poorest people. In recent years, countries in the north have paid for the construction of several huge dams. Every year between 1 and 2 million people are forced to leave their homes because dams flood their land. Power from dams provides electricity to run factories and light cities. Aid money that is spent on dams is seen to be an important step for countries that want to industrialize. In the short term, jobs are created building the dam and in the factories where the electricity generated by the dam is used. But these jobs are of little use to the people who have lost their land and livelihoods.

However, it would be wrong to dismiss all aid. Many aid agencies such as Oxfam in the United States, Canada, and Great Britain, NOVIB in Norway, and the United Nation's Children's Fund fill some of the gaps that are left by governments. The amount of aid they give is small in comparison, but it goes a long way. Aid agencies work to help poor people help themselves.

Helping people help themselves
In Bangladesh, it is unusual for women to go to work, so it is hard for them to earn money.

Dams built with aid money, like this one in Ghana, may provide power and store water for irrigation. But the poor, who have lost their land, are unlikely to share in the benefits of modern technology.

Local organizations, with help from aid agencies, have set up cooperatives so that women can make livings in their own homes. Thousands of women are weaving bags, mats, and hanging baskets from jute, a strong natural fiber that grows in Bangladesh. The women's work has helped them escape poverty. They have also gained independence and confidence. Many have begun to branch out into other areas, too, and are learning to read and write.

Wherever they live, the poor are no less capable than the rich. They only need to be given a fair chance. In the same way, poor countries need to be given a chance to escape the poverty trap.

Other solutions to the rich–poor divide

Other solutions have been suggested to end the rich–poor divide between countries. One of these is to redistribute wealth by taxation. The United Nations has suggested that the richest countries pay a tax of 0.1 percent of their gross national product.

Making hanging baskets from jute has allowed poor women in Bangladesh to support themselves. Women earn about 150 taka (about $5.00 per month). This does not solve all their economic problems, but it does keep them from extreme poverty.

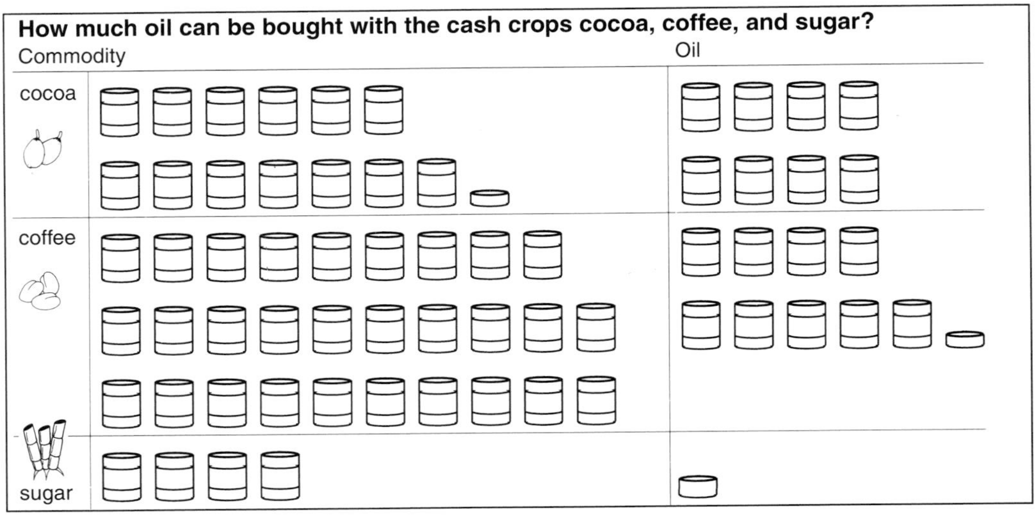

How much oil can be bought with the cash crops cocoa, coffee, and sugar?

Commodity | Oil

cocoa

coffee

sugar

Media Watch

Some different views on aid:

"Foreign aid is a method by which the United States maintains a position of influence and control around the world."

President John F. Kennedy

"Let us remember that the main purpose of American aid is not to help other nations but to help ourselves."

President Richard M. Nixon, in a 1968 election speech

"We do not want charity because it demeans. You cannot demand what you need from people who are helping you."

Mazide Ndiaye, RADI (a development organization based in Senegal, West Africa)

Fact File

Fair trade?
If you buy a pound of coffee in a supermarket for $3.50, less than 30 cents of what you pay will go to the farmer in the south who grew the coffee. The rest is divided among the importers, shippers, processors, and storeowners. More and more farmers in the south are demanding to be paid a fairer price for their work.

This would mean that about $20 billion a year would be available to divide among the poorest countries. It would be enough to provide basic health care and safe drinking water to all the world's people, provided that the money is spent where it is needed.

There are many possible ways to close the rich–poor divide. But none of them will work unless there is an urge to share. And that will only come about when individuals and countries learn to respect one another and care about one another's needs.

Our world is not such a huge place. Every day we are linked to people in many different countries, even though we might never have met them. The food we eat, the clothes we wear, and the television sets we watch may all come from the south. We all depend on each other for what we need. That's why it's up to all of us to do something—whether by writing to a newspaper or a congressman, donating time or money to a charity, or working to end discrimination or poverty in your town—to close the rich–poor divide.

Young people everywhere are trying to find answers to some of the problems that confront the world.

GLOSSARY

absolute poverty Not having enough to meet basic needs such as food, water, or shelter.

aid agency An organization that gives advice, money, or other help aimed at improving people's living conditions. Many aid agencies are charities.

birth rate The number of babies born in one year per 1,000 people in the population.

cash crops Crops grown to be sold for money and exported, not to be used by the people that have grown them. Tea and tobacco are common cash crops.

colony A country or people that is taken over or controlled by another country.

consumption The buying and using of goods or resources.

cooperative An organization formed by a group of people who share in its planning and running, as well as its profits or losses.

death rate The number of people who die in one year per 1,000 people in the population.

debt repayment The amount of money to be repaid on a loan.

discrimination Treating people unfairly because of negative feelings about their skin color, language, religion, or political beliefs.

donor country A country that gives aid to another country.

drought A shortage of rain that continues over a long period of time.

famine An extreme shortage of food in an area or country.

foreign investment Money lent by banks or the state in one country and sent to another.

gross national product (GNP) The total value of goods and services in a country. It is commonly used to measure the wealth of a country.

illiterate Being unable to read or write.

immunization Protection against certain diseases or infections such as whooping cough, polio, or measles.

indigenous peoples The first or original people who live in an area.

industrial revolution The period from about 1760 (in Europe) when industry was introduced and developed on a large scale.

informal economy The part of the economy and work that is not recognized by the state. Because it is not recognized, working conditions in the informal economy are often poor.

interest rates When people or countries lend money they expect to get back more than they lend. The extra is called interest. How much interest they get depends on the interest rates, which are usually expressed as a certain percentage of the money lent.

life expectancy The length of time a person can expect to live.

literacy Being able to read, write, and perform basic arithmetic.

malnutrition Not having enough of the right kind of food to stay healthy.

migration Moving from one area or country to another to work or settle.

newly industrializing countries A group of countries in the south whose manufacturing industries have grown very quickly in recent years. India, Indonesia, Brazil, and the Philippines are all newly industrializing countries.

per capita For each person. This figure is often used to measure averages. For example, GNP per capita is the amount of a country's GNP divided by its number of people.

population density The number of people living in an area of land. Cities have high population densities. Rural areas usually have low ones.

raw materials Materials that are used to make something else. Wood, oil, cotton, and minerals such as coal or gold are all raw materials.

relative poverty Not having enough to be able to lead a full life compared to other people in the community.

sanitation Arrangements to improve health; for example, providing clean water and drains to dispose of waste.

shantytown A town, or section of a town, where poor people live in self-built huts.

tied aid Aid that is given with strings attached. The donor countries may dictate how that money is spent.

United Nations An organization set up in 1945 to meet and discuss world issues in order to keep world peace and stop wars. Its members include almost all the world's countries.

universal affluence The appearance that all the people in a group or nation are rich.

urbanization The growth of cities caused either by population growth or by migration from the countryside.

World Bank An organization set up in 1944 to lend money to countries to pay for development projects.

USEFUL ADDRESSES

Food for the Hungry, P.O. Box E, Scottsdale, AZ 85260
    Telephone: (800) 248-6437
Interaction, 1717 Massachusetts Avenue NW, 8th Floor, Washington, DC 20036
    Telephone: (202) 667-8227
National Student Campaign Against Hunger and Homelessness, 29 Temple Place,
    Boston, MA 02111
    Telephone: (617) 292-4823
Oxfam America, 26 West Street, Boston, MA 02111-1206
    Telephone: (800) 225-5800
UNICEF International Headquarters, 3 UN Plaza, New York, NY 10017
    Telephone: (212) 326-7000
United Nations Development Program, 1 UN Plaza, New York, NY 10017
    Telephone: (212) 906-5000

FURTHER READING

Aaseng, Nathan. *Overpopulation: Crisis or Challenge?* New York: Franklin Watts, 1991.
Burby, Liza N. *World Hunger.* Overview Series. San Diego: Lucent Books,1994.
Davis, Bertha. *Poverty in America: What We Do About It.* Impact Books. New York:
    Franklin Watts, 1991.
DeKoster, Katie and Leone, Bruno, eds. *Poverty: Opposing Viewpoints.* San Diego:
    Greenhaven, 1994.
Fisher, Maxine P. *Women in the Third World.* New York: Franklin Watts, 1989.
Kerrod, Robin. *Food Resources.* World's Resources. New York: Thomson Learning,
    1994.
Lambert, David. *The World's Population.* Young Geographer. New York: Thomson
    Learning, 1993.
Nichaelson, Margery G. *Homeless or Hopeless?* Pro/Con. Minneapolis: Lerner
    Publications, 1994.
O'Toole, Thomas. *Global Economics.* Economics for Today. Minneapolis: Lerner
    Publications, 1990.
Pollard, Michael. *The United Nations.* Organizations that Help the World. New
    York: New Discovery Books, 1995.
Reed-King, Susan. *Food and Farming.* Young Geographer. New York: Thomson
    Learning, 1993.
Rohr, Janelle, ed. *Third World: Opposing Viewpoints.* San Diego: Greenhaven, 1989.
Stefoff, Rebecca. *Overpopulation.* Earth at Risk. New York: Chelsea House, 1992.
Swallow, Su. *Food for the World.* Facing the Future. Milwaukee: Raintree Steck-
    Vaughn, 1991.

INDEX